Show me how to
Plan My Quilting

■ DESIGN BEFORE YOU PIECE ■ A FUN NO-MARK APPROACH

Kathy Sandbach

C&T PUBLISHING

Text copyright © 2007 by Kathy Sandbach

Artwork copyright © 2007 by C&T Publishing, Inc.

Publisher: Amy Marson

Editorial Director: Gailen Runge

Acquisitions Editor: Jan Grigsby

Editor: Deb Rowden

Technical Editors: Helen Frost, Teresa Stroin

Proofreader/Copyeditor: Wordfirm Inc.

Cover Designer/Book Designer: Kristy K. Zacharias

Illustrator: Kirstie L. Pettersen

Production Coordinator: Kirstie L. Pettersen

Photography: Luke Mulks, Diane Pedersen unless otherwise noted

Published by C&T Publishing, Inc., P.O. Box 1456, Lafayette, CA, 94549

Library of Congress Cataloging-in-Publication Data

Sandbach, Kathy.

  Show me how to plan my quilting : design before you piece, a fun, no-mark approach / Kathy Sandbach.

    p. cm.

  Includes index.

  ISBN-13: 978-1-57120-428-8 (paper trade : alk. paper)

  ISBN-10: 1-57120-428-8 (paper trade : alk. paper)

  1. Quilting--Patterns. 2. Patchwork--Patterns. I. Title.

  TT835.S264 2007

  746.46'041--dc22

                          2006038228

Printed in China

10 9 8 7 6 5 4 3 2 1

Dedication

This book is dedicated to the two most important people in my life: my son, Ken, and my daughter, Kristine. Their support and confidence in their mom is an amazing gift to me.

Acknowledgments

I continue to appreciate my loyal customers for giving me the freedom to create designs on their quilts. Special thanks go to Diana McClun and Laura Nownes for their continued confidence in my work.

Table of Contents

CHAPTER 1

Show Me How to Plan My Quilting

The Basic Premise

My goal for this book is to encourage you to consider the quilting, the stitching in-the-ditch, and the overall appearance of your quilting design from the very beginning. Most quiltmakers choose pattern designs and fabrics without giving any thought to the quilting design. However, your quilt will be enhanced if you consider the quilting from the outset. Plan spaces to showcase quilting, or leave some piecing out to allow for visible quilting. It is very rewarding to plan the quilting and have a finished piece that is beautifully pieced or appliquéd and *perfectly quilted*.

Fabric Choices

Fabric choices affect the quilting process in very important ways. Large, busy prints or fabrics with extreme contrast (light/dark) will not allow the quilting to shine through. Contrasting pieces or several small pieces of differing color will also make the quilting almost impossible to see. For the quilting to show, the fabric pattern must look to the eye like a solid or almost solid (like a slightly mottled fabric). This does not mean you can't use a lovely large print in your quilt. Simply add a few fabrics that are solid or close to solid. Gail Sheirbon's quilt, *Purple Roses*, on page 37 is a perfect example of great fabric choices.

Thread Color

Thread color choices are also very important. A contrasting thread or a number of contrasting threads will be visible on solids or almost solids. Generally, white thread on white will allow the shadowing of the quilting to show.

Remember, areas you quilt will lie down, and areas you don't quilt will stand up. You always want to quilt the background more heavily than the foreground.

If you are not quilting the background more heavily, then strive for a balance of quilting in both background and foreground. If you want the quilting to really come forward and be visible from the background, use a contrasting thread. If you only want the background to recede, a like-colored thread will add texture and weight but not stand out and distract from the foreground.

Creating Empty Spaces for Quilting

Plan some empty spaces in your quilt design. No piecing and less appliqué will create space to display quilting. All the projects in this book have open spaces created specifically to show off quilting.

Pressing

In most of my quilts, and in most of the pieces that I quilt for others, I do a lot of quilting in-the-ditch, or what I often refer to as ditching. Stitching in the seams will make them lie down, as opposed to standing up. Although many quilters suggest opening seams when you press, doing so does not create a ditch. If you plan to stitch in-the-ditch, then the seams must be pressed to one side.

Thinking about the pressing as you make the quilt will help you choose a thread color for the ditch stitching. In patchwork, pieces with several seams are usually pressed toward a connecting piece with fewer or no seams, such as a pieced border seam being pressed toward a background piece. However, if the seam is pressed toward the pieced border, the background piece can be stitched using matching thread. This is easier than trying to pick a color that will look good on several different fabrics. Plan the best spot for stitching, and then press accordingly.

Open Spaces

To make it possible for the quilting to be visible, consider doing less piecing or using fewer pieces. Patty Black's *President's Quilt #1* on page 38 is a good example. Contributor Margaret Miller pieced the center with all beige fabrics, creating an open space. Margaret used darker fabrics to frame the other blocks. She framed the appliquéd blocks in light-colored fabric, allowing me to showcase the quilting.

Even in traditional pieces, the quilting will become more visible and integral to the overall look when some blocks are not pieced or appliquéd. Consider leaving every other block empty for a quilted feathered wreath, a quilted flower, or a quilted clone replicating the pattern in your print.

Cloning Designs

When contemplating fabrics, consider choosing one with a lovely big flower, a bonnet, an animal, or something that you can clone in the quilting. Consider *Dogwoods in Bloom* on page 11 or the *Purple Roses* quilt on page 37 by Gail Sheirbon. The quilting on Gail's quilt is roses and rose leaves, cloned from the beautiful purple roses on the fabric. An almost-solid batik was added to showcase the quilting.

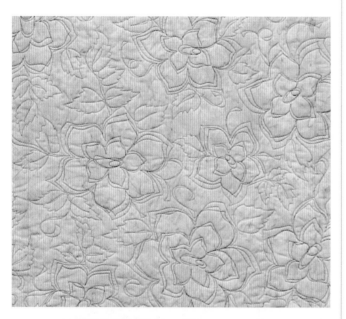

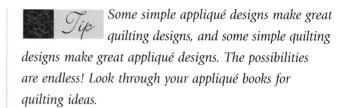

Tip Some simple appliqué designs make great quilting designs, and some simple quilting designs make great appliqué designs. The possibilities are endless! Look through your appliqué books for quilting ideas.

Special Effects

Trapunto, beads, ribbons, buttons, charms, or dimensional appliqué can create really wonderful special effects on a quilt.

The feather design is wonderful for using trapunto, or stuffed work. *Tulip Wreath* on page 41 and *Grape Wreath* on page 42 both have trapunto. The grape wreath has a cluster of grapes and large grape leaves with extra stuffing.

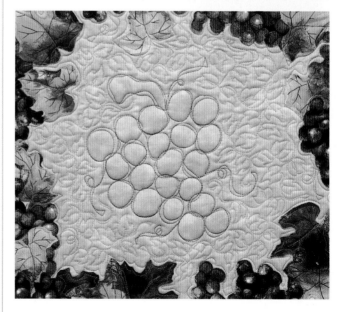

Children's Wallhanging on page 26 has yarn for the kite tails. In a quilt for older children, the use of buttons to enhance faces or to embellish baskets would be a great addition.

Christmas Table Runner and *Placemat* by Susie Robbins on page 32 are greatly enhanced with dimensional appliqué. *Strawberries on the Vine* on page 22 has small seed beads in place of seeds on the berries. It uses clear beads on the quilted berries and red beads on the appliquéd ones.

 *Do not embellish until after the quilting is done.*

Showcasing the Quilting

Blocks that run together or are similar in color can also showcase quilting. For the quilting to show, think in terms of solid fabrics or fabrics that read as solids. Consider eliminating lattice strips so corners of blocks create lovely, large areas to showcase quilting.

My basic philosophy is that *quilting is an integral part of the quilt.* Its purpose is to enhance what has been

pieced or appliquéd, not just to hold the layers together. Both *Dogwoods in Bloom* on page 11 and *Strawberries on the Vine* on page 22 showcase quilting in empty spaces.

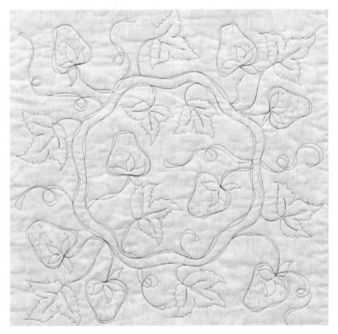

Deciding on the designs is easy! Just think of adding more of what is already there—either appliquéd or pieced.

How about spaces between appliqué left open just for the quilting? *Children's Wallhanging* on page 26 is a great example. Remember, for quilting to show in these spaces, use a contrasting thread. Just clone the designs that you have appliquéd!

I use lots of double-line quilting to convey the basic shape of the quilted design and create visual interest. These lines are not parallel; they are made by crossing a second line of stitching back and forth over the first. This creates a flowing, "ribboned" effect. It also makes the quilting more visible.

Throughout all the quilting, think simple! It doesn't need to be a very complicated design—just more cars, more kites, more boats, more flowers, or more leaves.

Simple designs are easy to draw and easy to quilt. As long as you capture the basic essence of the design, the quilting can be quite simple. Flowers, leaves, fruits, and vegetables, as well as cars, trucks, pitchers, and cups—you only need to consider the basic shapes. I really think simpler looks better. Drawings of how I quilted each quilt are at the back of the book. You can quilt yours the same way or any way you choose. The shapes don't need lots of detail to look great! If the quilting is too heavy with intricate quilting designs, then your quilt will become stiff in that spot and will shrink just in that area.

A Few Hints About Basics

■ Be sure you face your body square to your needle. Doing so will help your comfort level a great deal.

■ Lower your chair or raise your machine so you are looking out at your work, *not* down. Sharply bending your neck will contribute to stiffness and fatigue. Lower your chair a bit at a time, until you are comfortable looking out at your work.

Threads and More

My favorite thread continues to be Aurifil's Mako cotton in a 50 weight. I do a great deal of double stitching, and the lighter-weight thread works wonderfully. It is a high-quality thread with over 1,400 yards on a spool. This very strong 50-weight thread is always in my bobbin, even when clear or smoke nylon is on top. It looks great on the back of the quilt.

I wear gripper gloves (see Resources on page 61) whenever I am quilting. They help move the fabric smoothly and allow my hands to be the "hoop" that holds the quilt flat and taut. I do not recommend using any gloves that do not have the little rubber knobs all over the fingers and the palms, as this design allows better control of your work.

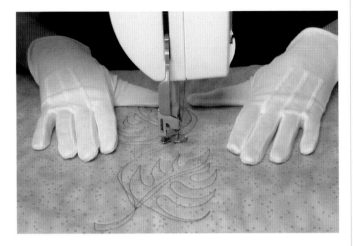

Christmas Table Runner and *Placemat* on page 32 were both quilted with Sulky Sliver. Sewer's Aid thread lubricant was put directly on the thread, which helped keep it from breaking. This flat thread, I believe, is the most dazzlingly visible—and that is what glitter is all about!

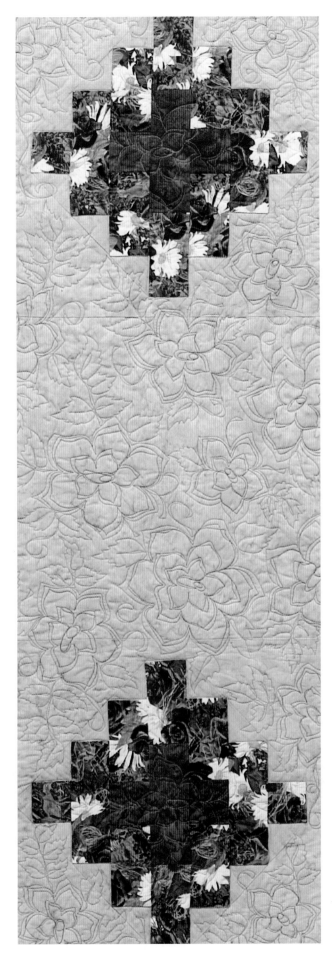

CHAPTER 2

Projects

Here are six projects for you to try. Each was designed with the quilting in mind. To showcase the quilting, these projects feature open spaces in the form of plain blocks or backgrounds. By planning the quilting, it becomes an integral part of the design.

Dogwoods in Bloom, by Kathy Sandbach, 2005. Quilt size: $58\frac{1}{2}'' \times 68''$

Photo by Gregory Case.

Fabrics

Black solid—3½ yards for background and borders

Yellow dotted—1 yard for flower centers, setting pieces, and binding

Medium light brown—1 yard for vines

Green—1 yard for leaves

White—¾ yard for petals

Backing—3¾ yards (pieced widthwise)

Batting—63″ × 73″

Cutting

Black solid:

Cut 5 lengthwise pieces 9″ × 54½″ for background.

Cut 2 lengthwise pieces 7″ × 55½″ for borders.

Cut 2 lengthwise pieces 7″ × 59″ for borders.

Yellow dotted:

Cut 11 strips 1⅛″ wide for setting pieces.

Cut 7 strips 2¼″ wide for binding.

Medium light brown:

Cut 6 strips 1⅛″ wide on fabric bias. Begin cutting at a corner to yield long strips. (There will be leftover fabric.)

Appliqué

All appliqué was done by hand. The patterns include seam allowances. If you prefer to fuse the appliqué pieces, eliminate these allowances.

1. Cut 36 petals, 9 centers, and 70 leaves.

2. For the vines, fold the medium light brown bias strips wrong sides together, and sew using a ⅛″ seam. Press the strips, centering the seamline on the back.

3. Appliqué the vines, flowers, flower centers, and leaves on 3 of the 9″ × 54½″ black pieces. Vary the placement of all the appliqué pieces. (See the quilt photo on page 11 for placement ideas.)

Piecing

1. Sew yellow dotted setting strips between the black background and appliquéd pieces, seaming the strips as necessary. Press the seams toward the yellow dotted strips.

2. Sew yellow dotted setting strips to the top and bottom. Press toward the yellow dotted strips.

3. Sew yellow dotted setting strips to the sides. Press toward the yellow dotted strips.

Tip *Cut 1⅛″-wide strips for ½″-wide finished pieces. The extra ⅛″ compensates for the folding and pressing of the seams.*

Borders

1. Sew the 7″ × 55½″ black border pieces to the sides. Press toward the yellow dotted strips.

2. Sew the 7″ × 59″ black border pieces to the top and bottom. Press toward the yellow dotted strips.

3. Appliqué the vines and leaves to the borders.

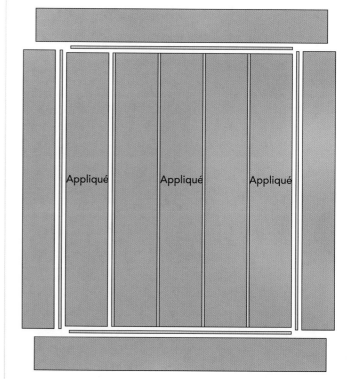

Piecing diagram

Quilting

Layer the top on the batting and backing fabric. Use small safety pins to baste the layers together. Refer to the quilt photo on page 11 and the quilting designs on page 44. Quilt the flowers with white thread, using double-line quilting. Change to yellow thread to quilt the centers, making sure to quilt lots of small circles. Add the vines in brown thread, and then add the leaves along the edges. I also quilted a few dogwood flowers on the border.

Bind.

Tip *If you have trouble quilting the flower designs, try cutting the shapes from freezer paper. Touch the iron to the paper to make the paper lightly adhere to the top of the quilt. Then simply quilt around the outside edges of the paper.*

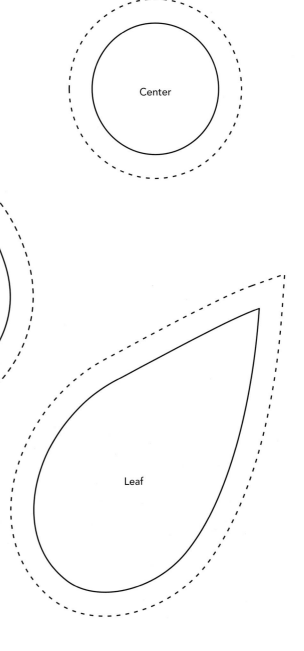

Center

Petal

Leaf

Patterns for *Dogwoods in Bloom*

Fall in Oregon, by Kathy Sandbach, 2006. Quilt size: 42″ × 54″.
My thanks to Sue Rasmussen for the tree quilting inspiration.

Fabrics

Assorted beige prints—$1/4$ yard each of 12 fabrics for background

Brown—2 yards for tree and binding

Green, gold, and rust prints—$1/8$ yard each of 6 fabrics for leaves

Backing—3 yards (pieced widthwise)

Batting—47″ × 59″

Lightweight fusible web—$1/2$ yard

Embroidery thread—6 skeins of dark brown to match tree fabric

Cutting

Assorted beige prints:

Cut 126 rectangles $3^{1}/_{2}″ \times 6^{1}/_{2}″$ for appliqué background.

Brown:

Cut 6 strips $2^{1}/_{4}″$ wide for binding.

Piecing

1. Sew the rectangles together on the long sides. Make 7 rows, each with 18 rectangles.

2. Press the seams of each row in opposite directions.

3. Sew the rows together. Press.

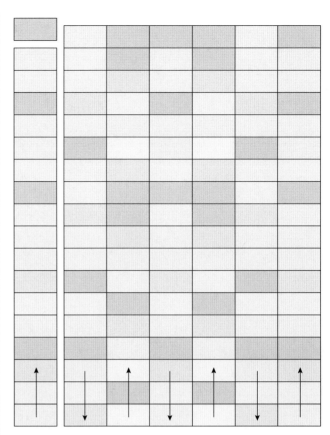

Background piecing diagram: Arrows indicate pressing direction.

Appliqué

1. Use the tree diagram on page 16 for the tree shape. Stitch in place using either hand or machine appliqué; I chose to hand appliqué it.

2. Embroider the small "branches" using 3 strands of embroidery thread. Use 3 rows of stitching where the branches meet the tree, and taper down to 1 row at the tips.

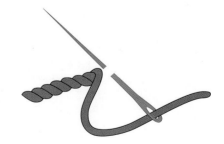

3. Cut 44 leaves. Use $\frac{1}{2}$″-wide strips of lightweight fusible web down the middle of the leaves so the edges are loose. Fuse the leaves in place, following the quilt photo on page 14 or your own design.

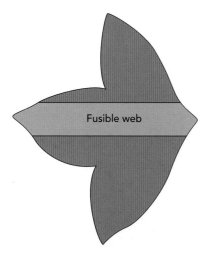

Apply fusible web to center back side of leaf.

Quilting

Layer the top on the batting and backing fabric. Use small safety pins to baste the layers together. The quilting echoes the branches. Refer to the quilt photo on page 14 and the quilting designs on page 45. Add small double-line quilted twigs to fill the background spaces where needed, and outline the leaves and stitch the veins. I added a few quilted leaves to fill the background. In addition, I quilted fallen leaves into small branches at the bottom. I quilted the tree with a jagged line and echoed the printed knots in the fabric.

Bind.

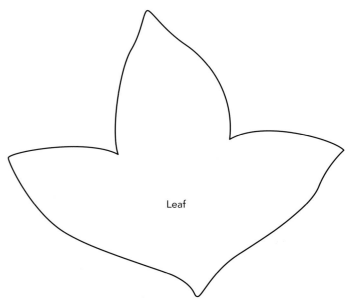

Pattern for *Fall in Oregon*

1 square = 2″

Tree diagram

Tea Time, by Kathy Sandbach, 2006. Quilt size: 54˝ × 70˝

Fabrics

Note *Pick a fabric that shows distinct items. It could be teapots and cups, teddy bears, trucks, houses, and so forth. Your quilt may be slightly different, depending on what you frame. Patterns are provided so you can create your own teapots and cups from different fabrics.*

Teapot print—1 yard or enough yardage to yield 9 motifs

Bright solids and prints—$1/2$ yard each of 8 fabrics for backgrounds and border

Black background dotted—2 yards total of 3 fabrics for block frames, border, and binding

White background dotted—$1 1/2$ yards for block frames and border

Bright pink—$1 1/2$ yards for setting pieces and border

Backing—$3 1/2$ yards (pieced widthwise)

Batting—$59'' \times 75''$

Lightweight fusible web—$1 1/4$ yards

Cutting

Bright solids and prints:
Cut 4 rectangles $9'' \times 7''$ for appliquéd cup backgrounds.

Cut 5 rectangles $11'' \times 9''$ for appliquéd teapot backgrounds.

Cut 4 rectangles $8 1/2'' \times 6 1/2''$ for quilted cup backgrounds.

Cut 1 rectangle $9 1/2'' \times 13 1/2''$ for quilted teapot background.

Cut a total of 8 strips $2 1/2''$ wide; then cut into $2 1/2''$ squares for border.

Black background dotted:
Cut 15 strips $1 1/2''$ wide for block inner frames.

Cut 2 strips $2''$ wide for quilted teapot block frames.

Cut 4 strips $2 1/2''$ wide; then cut into $2 1/2''$ squares for border.

Cut 7 strips $2 1/4''$ wide for binding.

White background dotted:
Cut 17 strips $2 1/2''$ wide for block outer frames.

Cut 1 strip $2 1/2''$ wide; then cut into $2 1/2''$ squares for border.

Bright pink:
Cut 10 strips $3''$ wide for setting pieces.

Cut 6 strips $1 1/2''$ wide for inner border.

Cut 2 strips $2 1/2''$ wide; then cut into $2 1/2''$ squares for border.

Appliqué

1. All appliqué is done with lightweight fusible web. Fuse the web onto the back side of the fabric, and cut out the motifs exactly on the lines.

2. If you are using the patterns, trace them on the paper side of the web. Cut around the shapes, leaving $1/4''$ outside the lines. Fuse the web to the back side of the appliqué fabrics, and cut out the designs exactly on the lines.

3. Peel off the paper, and fuse the designs in place on the background fabrics.

4. Cut and fuse 4 cup and 5 teapot motifs.

5. Stitch in place, using a blanket stitch and coordinating thread.

Piecing

1. Sew the 2″ black background dotted strips to the background for the quilted teapot block. Sew the 1¹/₂″ black background dotted strips to the remaining blocks.

2. Sew the 2¹/₂″ white background dotted strips to the framed appliquéd blocks.

3. Trim the appliquéd cup blocks to 15″ × 12¹/₂″. For the center vertical row, trim 3 appliquéd teapot blocks to 15¹/₂″ × 13¹/₂″. For the side vertical rows, trim 2 appliquéd teapot blocks to 15″ × 13¹/₂″.

4. Trim the pieces for the quilted cup blocks to 10¹/₂″ × 8¹/₂″. Trim the piece for the quilted teapot to 12¹/₂″ × 16¹/₂″.

5. Your design wall is an important part of this project. Place the blocks on a design wall. Arrange them following the photo or as you like.

6. Sew the 3″ bright pink strips to the top and 1 side of 2 appliqué cup blocks and to the bottom and 1 side of 2 appliquéd cup blocks. Trim to 15″ × 13¹/₂″.

7. Sew a 3″ bright pink strip to the top of the center bottom appliquéd teapot block. Trim to 15¹/₂″ × 15¹/₂″.

8. Sew the 3″ bright pink strips to the quilted cup blocks. Trim to 15″ × 11″.

9. Sew the 3″ bright pink strips to the quilted teapot block. Trim to 15¹/₂″ × 19¹/₂″.

10. Sew the blocks into 3 vertical rows, with the center row measuring 15¹/₂″ × 60¹/₂″ and the side rows measuring 15″ × 60¹/₂″. Join the rows.

Borders

1. Border the joined rows with 1¹/₂″ bright pink strips, piecing the strips as needed. Sew to the top and bottom, and then to the sides, of the quilt top. Press.

2. Sew the 2¹/₂″ squares in pairs, trying not to put 2 squares of the same fabric next to each other. Press the seams in opposite directions.

3. Arrange and sew 31 pairs for each of the side borders. Arrange and sew 27 pairs for each of the top and bottom borders. Sew the side borders, and then the top and bottom borders, to the quilt top.

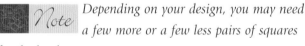 *Note* *Depending on your design, you may need a few more or a few less pairs of squares for the border.*

Quilting

Layer the top on the batting and backing fabric. Use small safety pins to baste the layers together. Refer to the quilt photo on page 17 and the quilting designs on pages 46–48. Stitch in-the-ditch on the block frames and around the appliquéd pieces using matching thread. Quilt the cup and teapot designs in the open blocks, using double-line quilting to create a ribboned effect. The big, quilted teapot in the center was outlined from a freezer-paper template. Details were added after removing the paper.

Quilt the backgrounds with echo quilting, abstract curves, or sticks and curls. Fill the white background dotted frames with shapes: squares, circles, diamonds, rectangles, and triangles. Quilt the black background dotted frames with a double ribbon design. In the bright pink areas, I quilted names of different types of teas, as well as the quilt name. Quilt the border squares diagonally in both directions. Remember to leave $1/4''$ on the outside edges for the binding seam allowance.

Finishing

Bind.

Cut the strings and labels from 19 teabags. Thread a needle with each string, and stitch through the quilt from the front. Knot the strings on the back of the quilt.

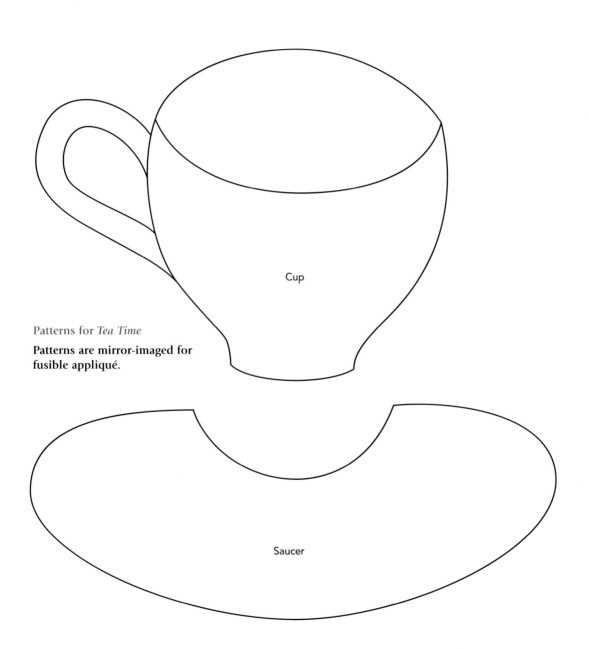

Patterns for *Tea Time*

Patterns are mirror-imaged for fusible appliqué.

Cup

Saucer

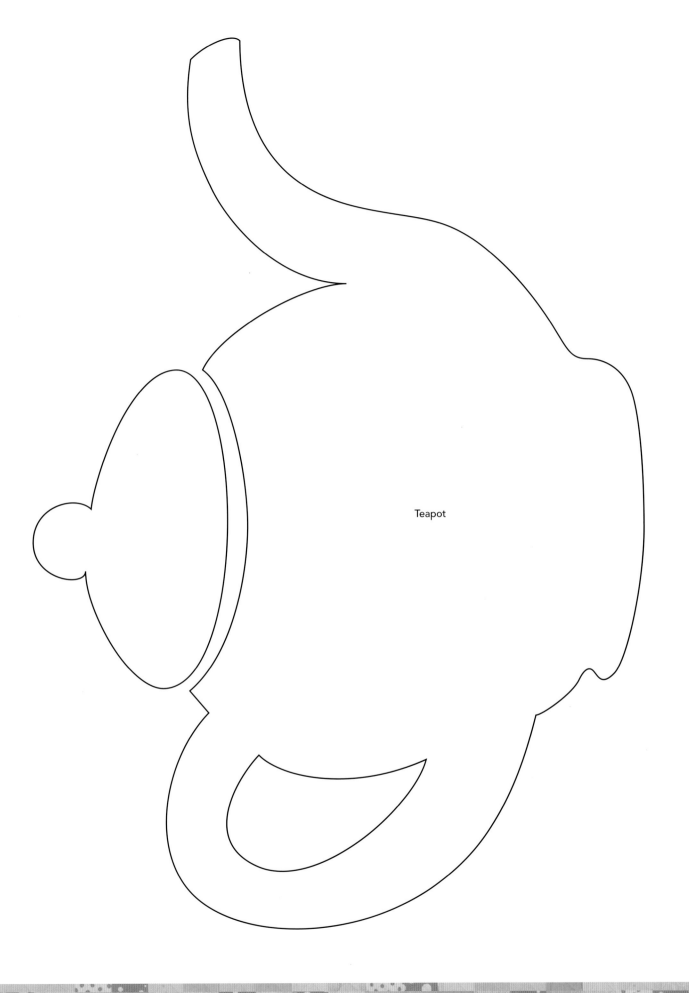

Teapot

Strawberries on the Vine, by Kathy Sandbach, 2006. Quilt size: 54˝ × 54˝

Fabrics

Pink—3 yards for background

Red—2 yards for block frames, strawberries, and binding

Green—1¹/₂ yards for vines, strawberry caps, and leaves

Backing—3¹/₂ yards

Batting—61″ × 61″

Lightweight fusible web—3 yards

Seed beads—approximately 350 red and 275 clear

Cutting

Pink:

Cut 5 squares 17¹/₂″ × 17¹/₂″ for appliqué background.

Cut 4 squares 18¹/₂″ × 18¹/₂″ for quilting background.

Red:

Cut 10 strips 1¹/₈″ wide for block frames.

Cut 7 strips 4³/₄″ wide for binding.

Lightweight fusible web:

Cut 1 rectangle 7″ × 45″ for vines.

Appliqué

1. All appliqué is done with lightweight fusible web. Trace the patterns on the paper side of the web. Reverse some of the leaves and caps to add variety to your project. Cut around the shapes, leaving ¹/₄″ outside the lines.

2. Fuse the web to the back side of the appliqué fabrics, and cut out the designs exactly on the lines. Peel off the paper, and fuse the designs in place on the background fabric.

3. Cut and fuse 40 strawberries, 40 caps, and 135 leaves.

4. Place the 7″ × 45″ piece of fusible web across 1 corner of the back of the green fabric. Position it on the bias of the fabric, approximately 30″ from the corner on both the selvage and cut edges. Fuse it to the fabric. Cut 5 bias strips ¹/₂″ × 45″ and 10 bias strips ¹/₄″ × 45″.

5. Enlarge the placement diagram 235% (page 25). Trace the vine pattern onto the 17¹/₂″ squares, drawing a single line between the lines of the wavy circle.

6. Center the ¹/₂″-wide green strips for the vines over the wavy circle line, and fuse in place.

7. Position and fuse the ¹/₄″ strips for the stems and then the strawberries, caps, and leaves.

8. Coordinate the colors of the threads with the fabrics. Stitch in place using a blanket stitch for the vines and strawberries and a machine feather stitch for the leaves.

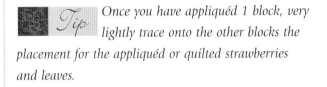 *Tip* *Once you have appliquéd 1 block, very lightly trace onto the other blocks the placement for the appliquéd or quilted strawberries and leaves.*

Piecing

1. Sew the red strips to the appliquéd blocks. Press toward the red strips.

2. Arrange and sew the blocks into 3 rows. Press toward the red strips. Join the rows.

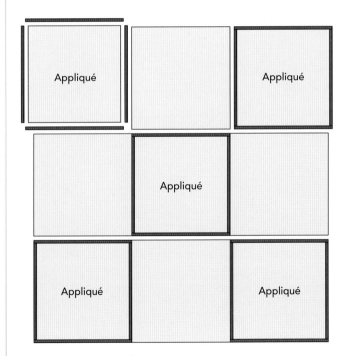

Frame appliquéd strawberry blocks with narrow red strips, and then piece into rows.

Quilting

Layer the top on the batting and backing fabric. Use small safety pins to baste the layers together. Refer to the quilt photo on page 22 and the quilting designs on page 49. Quilt in-the-ditch using pink thread. Quilt the appliqué blocks, using red around the strawberries and green thread for leaves, vines, and tendrils. Quilt the open blocks, again using red thread for the berries and green thread for everything else. I quilted twice around the center circle.

Finishing

Bind. The wide binding strips (cut 4³/₄″) make an approximately 1″-wide finished binding. Leave a large pleat (about ³/₄″) when stitching the corners of the binding so it will turn nicely.

After the quilt is entirely done, sew 8 or 9 seed beads to each of the strawberries. Use red beads on the appliquéd berries and clear beads on the quilted berries.

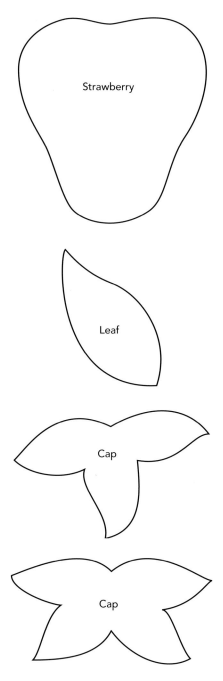

Patterns for *Strawberries on the Vine*

Vine placement and quilting design: Enlarge 235%.

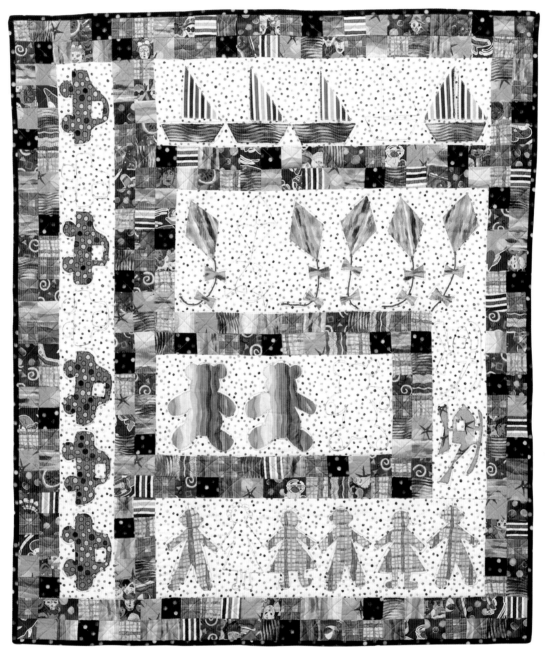

Children's Wallhanging, by Kathy Sandbach, 2006. Quilt size: 37$\frac{1}{2}$″ × 45″

Fabrics

White polka dot—1¼ yards for background

Bright prints—¼ yard each of 14 fabrics for appliqué and border

Black polka dot—¾ yard for border and binding

Backing—1½ yards

Batting—42″ × 50″

Lightweight fusible web—2 yards

Red yarn—2 yards for kite tails

Cutting

White polka dot:

Cut 1 rectangle 24½″ × 6½″ for boat appliqué background.

Cut 1 rectangle 23″ × 9½″ for kite appliqué background.

Cut 1 rectangle 17″ × 8″ for bear appliqué background.

Cut 1 rectangle 24½″ × 8″ for boy and girl appliqué background.

Cut 1 rectangle 14″ × 5″ for helicopter appliqué background.

Cut 1 rectangle 39½″ × 5″ for car appliqué background.

Bright prints:

Cut a total of 16 strips 2″ wide; then cut into 2″ squares for border.

Black polka dot:

Cut 2 strips 2″ wide; then cut into 2″ squares for border.

Cut 5 strips 2¼″ wide for binding.

Appliqué

1. All appliqué is done with lightweight fusible web. Trace the patterns on the paper side of the web. Cut around the shapes, leaving ¼″ outside the lines.

2. Fuse the web to the back side of the appliqué fabrics, and cut out the designs exactly on the lines. Peel off the paper, and fuse the designs in place on the background fabric.

3. Cut and fuse 4 boats (one with a double sail), 5 kites, 10 kite bows, 2 bears, 1 helicopter, 3 boys, 2 girls, and 5 cars.

4. Stitch in place, using a blanket stitch and coordinating thread.

Note   Fuse the kites, and then add the yarn tails, couching the red yarn. Fuse the bows on top of the yarn; then blanket stitch them in place.

Piecing

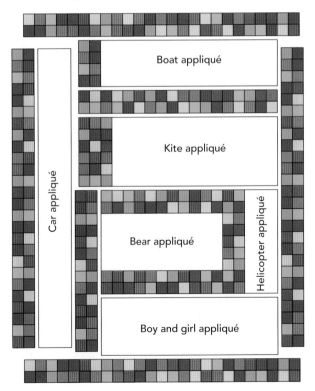

Assembly diagram

1. You will need a total of 356 squares for the checker-board borders. Use the assembly diagram as a guideline to arrange the squares, trying not to put 2 squares of the same fabric next to each other. Press the seams in opposite directions.

2. Sew 2 rows of 4 squares each to the left-hand edge of the boat appliqué piece.

3. Sew 3 rows of 6 squares each to the left-hand edge of the kite appliqué piece.

4. Sew together 2 rows of 18 squares each. Sew this between the boat and kite pieces.

5. Sew 2 rows of 11 squares each to the top and bottom edges of the bear appliqué piece. Sew 2 rows of 9 squares each to the right-hand edge of the bear appliqué piece. Add the helicopter appliqué piece to the right-hand edge; then add the boy and girl appliqué piece to the bottom edge.

6. Sew 2 rows of 14 squares each to the left-hand edge of the joined pieces from Step 5.

7. Join the sections from Steps 4 and 6.

8. Add the car appliqué section.

*Tip Pressing is important. When pressing, press the seams **away** from the background fabric. Then you can use 1 color of thread to stitch in-the-ditch on all the backgrounds.*

Patterns for *Children's Wallhanging*

Patterns are mirror-imaged for fusible appliqué.

Borders

1. Sew together 2 rows of 26 squares for each side border. Sew to the quilt top. Press toward the squares.

2. Sew together 2 rows of 25 squares for each of the top and bottom borders. Sew to the quilt top. Press toward the squares.

Quilting

Layer the top on the batting and backing fabric. Use small safety pins to baste the layers together. Refer to the quilt photo on page 26 and the patterns on pages 49–51. The quilting is very easy. Quilt in-the-ditch around the blocks. Stitch diagonally across the squares. Remember to leave 1/4″ on the outside edges for the binding seam allowance. Quilt around the appliquéd pieces with primary-colored variegated thread. Have fun adding hair to the kids' heads. Repeat the appliqué designs in the open spaces with navy blue thread.

Bind.

Tip Cut the quilting designs from freezer paper, gently press them in place, and then quilt just outside the edge of the paper.

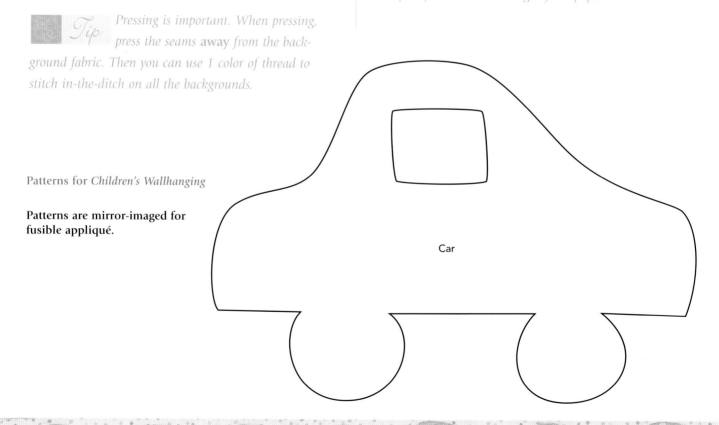

Car

Helicopter

Kite

Bear

Kite bow

Girl

Boy

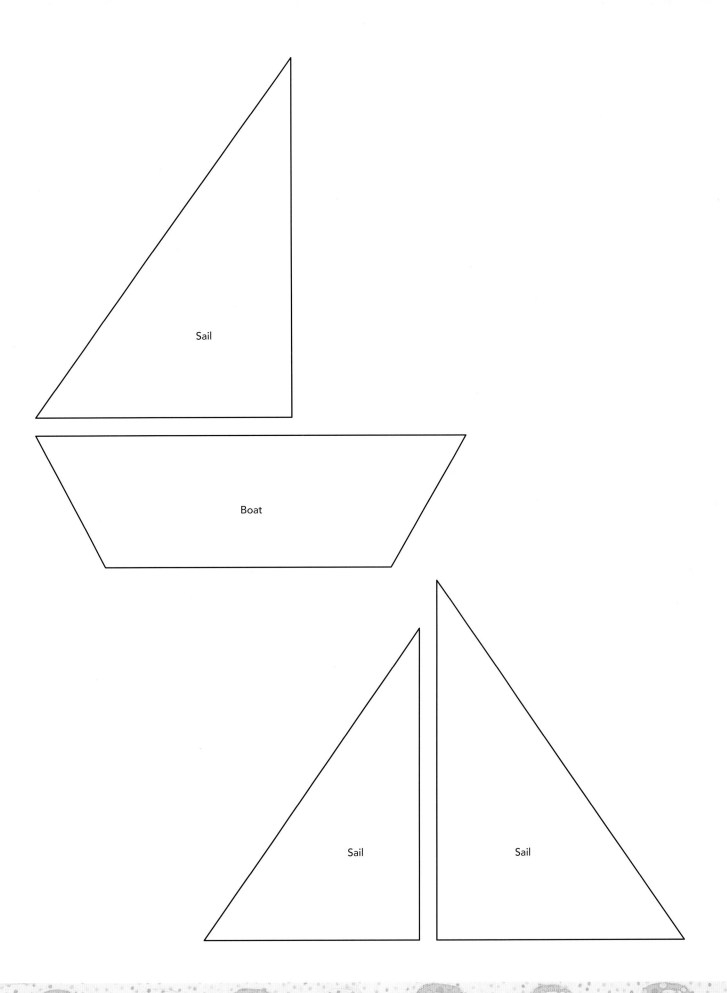

Sail

Boat

Sail

Sail

Christmas Placemat,
by Susie Robbins, 2006.
Size: 20˝ × 20˝

Christmas Table Runner,
by Susie Robbins, 2006.
Size: 70˝ × 18˝

Fabrics for Table Runner

Circular motif print—¼ yard for block center

Gold, red, light gold, and paisley prints—¼ yard each for block

Dark green—1¼ yards for setting triangles and appliqué background

Assorted greens—⅓ yard each of 5 fabrics for holly leaves

Green dot—½ yard for binding

Backing—1⅜ yards (pieced widthwise)

Batting—22″ × 74″

Lightweight fusible web—1 yard

Heart-shaped buttons—18 each in small, medium, and large sizes

Beads and bells for holly leaves

Cutting for Table Runner

Circular motif print:
Cut 1 square 4½″ × 4½″ (A).

Gold print:
Cut 8 squares 2½″ × 2½″ (B).

Cut 2 squares 3¼″ × 3¼″; then cut twice diagonally (G).

Red print:
Cut 8 squares 2⅞″ × 2⅞″; then cut once diagonally (C).

Light gold print:
Cut 8 squares 2⅞″ × 2⅞″; then cut once diagonally (D).

Cut 2 squares 3¼″ × 3¼″; then cut twice diagonally (F).

Paisley print:
Cut 4 squares 2⅞″ × 2⅞″; then cut once diagonally (E).

Dark green:
Cut 2 squares 12″ × 12″; then cut once diagonally (these are cut oversize).

Cut 2 rectangles 18″ × 26″ for appliqué and quilting background.

Green dot:
Cut 5 strips 2¼″ wide for binding.

Piecing for Table Runner

1. Arrange and sew the block pieces following the diagram. Sew together in rows. Join the rows.

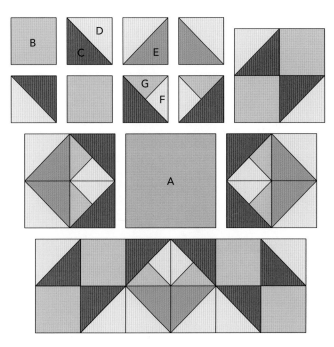

Center block for *Christmas Table Runner*

2. Center and sew the dark green triangles to the block. Press toward the triangles. Trim to 18″ × 18″.

3. Cut 1 end of each dark green rectangular piece at a 60° angle to form a point. Sew the pieces to the center. Press toward the rectangles.

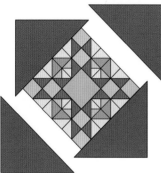

Table runner assembly diagram

Appliqué

1. All appliqué is done with lightweight fusible web. Trace the holly leaf pattern on the paper side of the web. Reverse some of the leaves to add variety. Cut around the shapes, leaving ¼″ outside the lines.

2. Fuse the web to the back side of the assorted green appliqué fabrics. Cut out the designs exactly on the lines. Peel off the paper, and fuse the designs in place on the background fabric. Refer to the photo on page 32.

3. Cut and fuse 10 holly leaves.

4. Stitch the holly with a blanket stitch and metallic thread.

Quilting

Layer the runner on the batting and backing fabric. Use small safety pins to baste the layers together. Refer to the table runner photo on page 32 and the quilting designs on pages 52–53. Stitch the center block in-the-ditch. Quilt the rest of the table runner with metallic thread. On each end, I quilted holly leaves in a circle to form a wreath, a large Christmas present in the center, and smaller presents to fill in the open spaces. I used trapunto on the leaves for dimension. I also quilted oblong holly berries. Susie added heart-shaped buttons to some of the quilted berries.

Bind.

Finishing

1. Make 3-dimensional holly leaves to accent the table runner. Trace the pattern for 16 leaves onto the wrong side of the assorted green fabrics. Cut out the shapes ½″ outside the lines.

2. Place each leaf on a matching piece of green fabric, right sides together, and cut to the same shape. Layer the pieces on top of a piece of batting.

3. Stitch on the marked line. Trim the excess fabric, leaving a scant ¼″ seam allowance.

4. Cut a slit in the top layer of fabric, and turn it right side out. The batting will be sandwiched between the layers.

5. Machine quilt around the edges, and stitch veins on each holly leaf. Embellish with beads and bells.

6. Placing the cut side down, lightly tack the leaves in place. Add 4 leaves at each end and 8 leaves around the center. Refer to the photo on page 32.

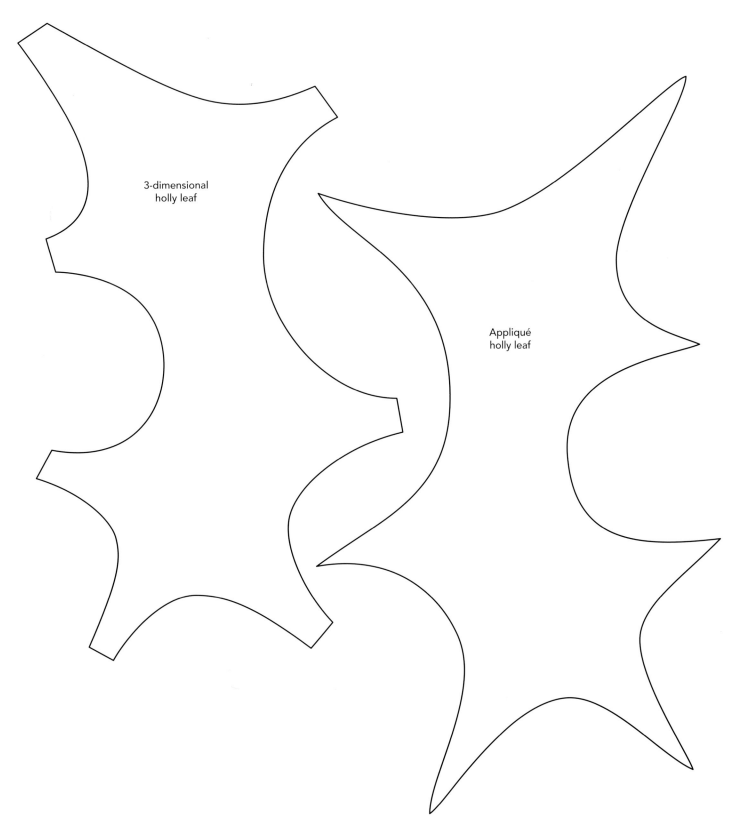

Patterns for *Christmas Table Runner*

3-dimensional
holly leaf

Appliqué
holly leaf

Fabrics for 2 Placemats

Circular motif print—$\frac{1}{4}$ yard for block center

Paisley print—$\frac{1}{2}$ yard for blocks

Small floral, gold, light gold, red, and green prints—$\frac{1}{4}$ yard each for blocks

Dark green—$\frac{3}{4}$ yard for setting triangles

Green dot—$\frac{1}{2}$ yard for binding

Backing—$1\frac{1}{2}$ yards

Batting—2 pieces 24″ × 24″

Cutting for Each Placemat

Circular motif print:
Cut 1 square $4\frac{1}{2}$″ × $4\frac{1}{2}$″ (A).

Paisley print:
Cut 4 squares $2\frac{1}{2}$″ × $2\frac{1}{2}$″ (B).

Cut 8 squares $2\frac{7}{8}$″ × $2\frac{7}{8}$″; then cut once diagonally (E).

Small floral print:
Cut 4 squares $2\frac{1}{2}$″ × $2\frac{1}{2}$″ (C).

Gold print:
Cut 8 squares $2\frac{7}{8}$″ × $2\frac{7}{8}$″; then cut once diagonally (D).

Light gold print:
Cut 4 squares $2\frac{7}{8}$″ × $2\frac{7}{8}$″; then cut once diagonally (F).

Red print:
Cut 2 squares $3\frac{1}{4}$″ × $3\frac{1}{4}$″; then cut twice diagonally (G).

Green print:
Cut 2 squares $3\frac{1}{4}$″ × $3\frac{1}{4}$″; then cut twice diagonally (H).

Dark green:
Cut 2 squares 12″ × 12″; then cut once diagonally (these are cut oversize).

Green dot:
Cut 3 strips $2\frac{1}{4}$″ wide for binding.

Piecing

1. Arrange and sew the block pieces following the diagram. Sew together in rows. Join the rows.

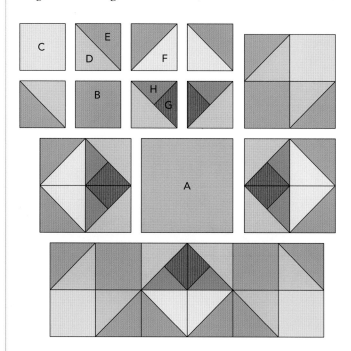

Center block for *Christmas Placemat*

2. Center and sew the dark green triangles to the block as shown in the table runner assembly diagram on page 34. Press toward the triangles. Trim to 20″ × 20″.

Quilting

Layer the placemats on the batting and backing fabric. Use small safety pins to baste the layers together. Refer to the placemat photo on page 32 and the quilting designs on page 52. Stitch the block in-the-ditch. Quilt holly leaves and berries in the triangles using metallic thread. Susie did not embellish the placemat.

Bind.

CHAPTER 3

Gallery Quilts

Purple Roses

61″ × 61″, by Gail Sheirbon of Saratoga, California; quilted by the author.

This design comes from Debby Kratovil's *Quilting Block & Pattern-a-Day Calendar*. Gail chose to add a solid border instead of the pieced border in the pattern. The large, open spaces are great for quilting roses and rose leaves.

President's Quilt #1

85″ × 85″, owned by Patricia L. Black of Rapid City, South Dakota; quilted by the author.

These blocks were gifts to Patricia from various members of the Minnesota Quilters Guild at the end of her yearlong tenure as president. The blocks were set into a quilt top by Margaret J. Miller of Bremerton, Washington, and machine quilted by the author.

Margaret used a light color for the center block frames, which made the backgrounds blend nicely and the quilting very visible. The author quilted more flowers and leaves, which add to the appliquéd flowers and leaves.

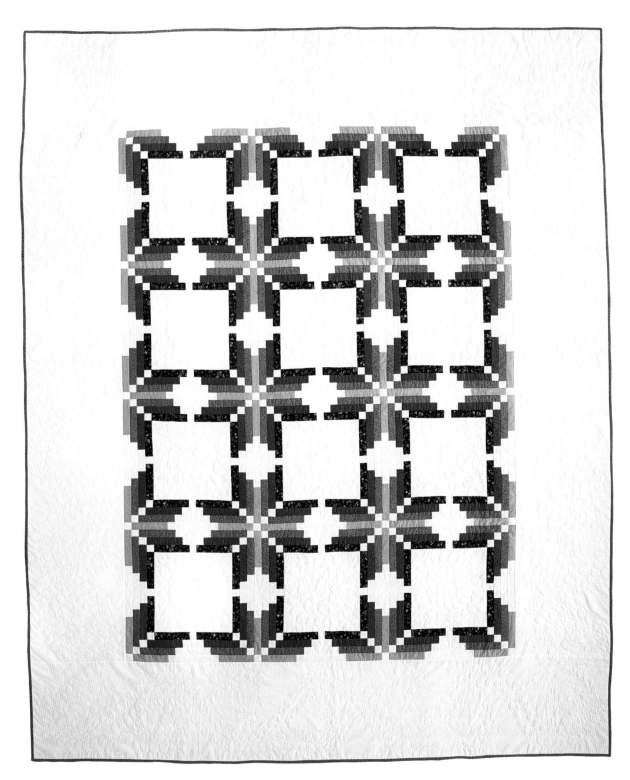

Striply Speaking

82″ × 100″, by Sue Coates of Kerrville, Texas; quilted by the author.

Sue stitched this quilt at an overnight retreat led by Kathy Thompson, using a mystery quilt pattern from Debbie Caffrey. The large, open spaces were perfect for feather quilting, and the large white border was a wonderful place to quilt the elaborate (but easy) border design.

Happy Holidays

41″ × 41″, by Ellen Garner of Rancho Cordova, California; quilted by the author.

In this quilt, Ellen fused the poinsettias and holly leaves. Large spaces allowed for more quilted foliage. The author used double stitching around the flowers and filled in the background with holly leaves. The center greeting, "Happy Holidays," was quilted around freezer-paper patterns of the words.

Tulip Wreath

52″ × 50″, by the author.

Flowers and leaves were fused and then quilted along the edges to keep them in place. The feathered wreath in the center and the feathers in the corners were created using trapunto. The background was quilted in a small leaf vine pattern.

Grape Wreath

24″ × 28″, by the author.

This is a great little wallhanging. A slightly jagged leaf pattern was used to heavily quilt the background behind the trapunto grape cluster in the center, as well as the leaves in the corners.

Susie's Magic Vine

61″ × 86″, by Susie Robbins of Bonita Springs, Florida; quilted by the author.

In a plan similar to the *Dogwoods in Bloom* quilt, Susie left small areas between her appliqué rows for the author to quilt. Susie then embellished the quilt with yo-yos. Sometimes you can add a great deal to a quilt simply by leaving open spaces available for quilting designs.

Quilting Designs

To use all of these designs, trace them onto freezer paper. Enlarge, shrink, and flip designs as necessary. Cut them out on the lines. Press the freezer paper shapes to the right side of the quilt top, and quilt following the outside of the shapes. Remove the freezer paper from the quilt, and reuse it if possible.

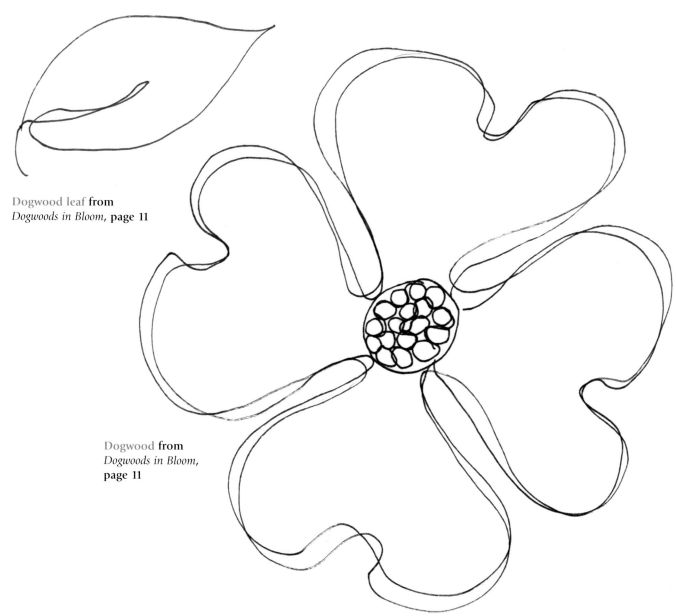

Dogwood leaf from
Dogwoods in Bloom, **page 11**

Dogwood from
Dogwoods in Bloom,
page 11

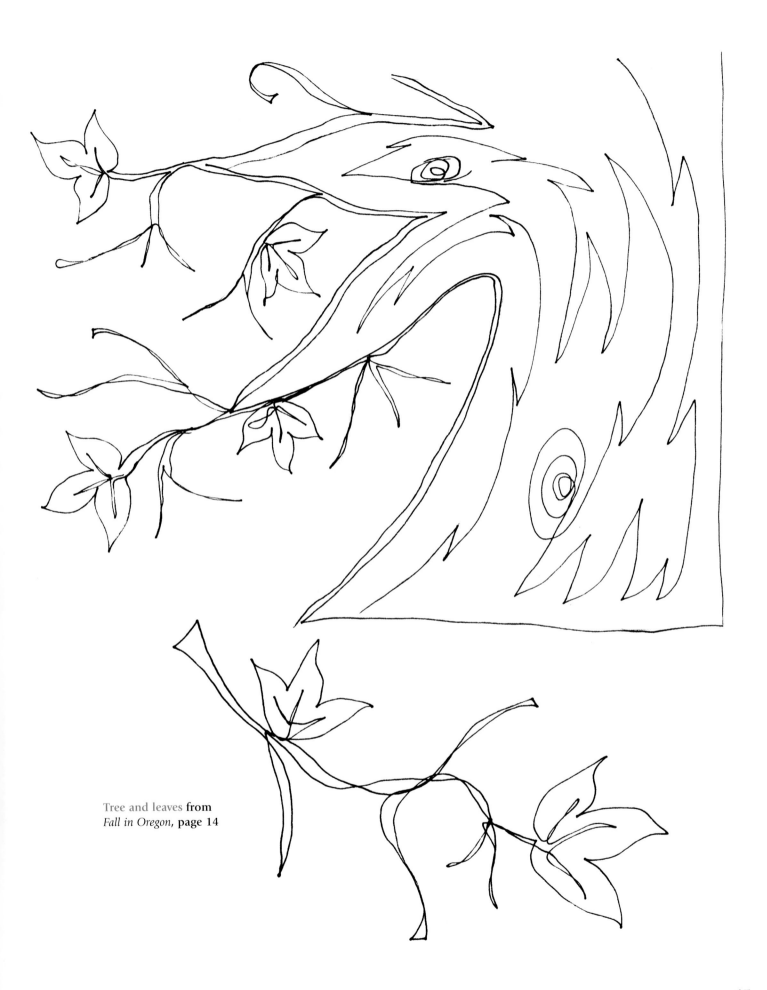

Tree and leaves from
Fall in Oregon, **page 14**

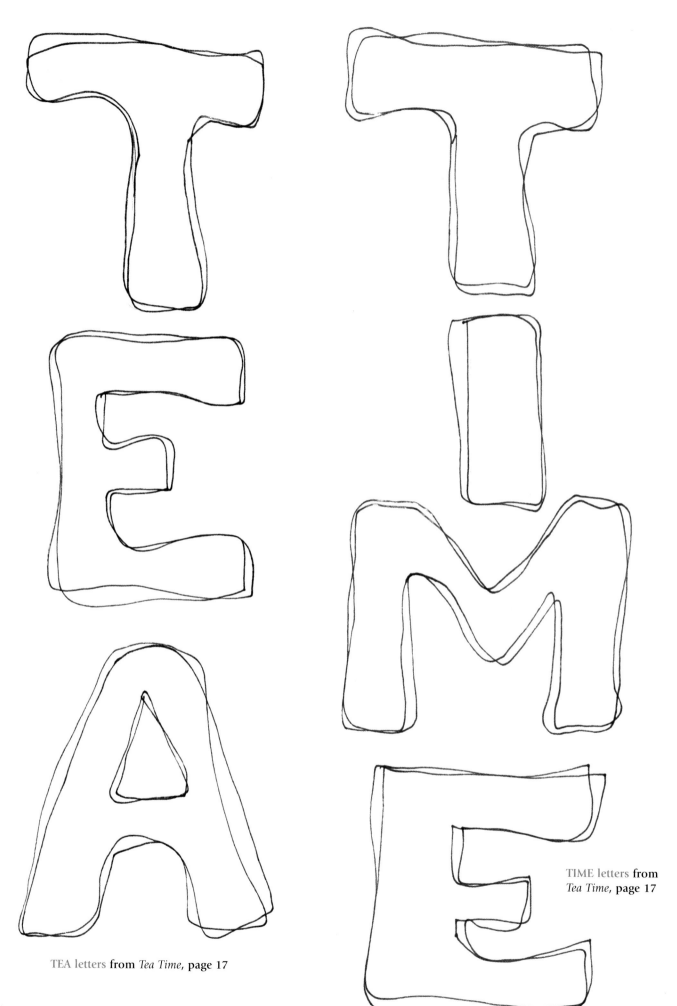

TEA letters from *Tea Time,* **page 17**

TIME letters from *Tea Time,* **page 17**

Big pot **from** *Tea Time*, **page 17**

Teacup **from** *Tea Time*, **page 17**

Coffee cup **from** *Tea Time*, **page 17**

Strawberry **from**
Strawberries on the Vine,
page 22

Strawberry leaf **from**
Strawberries on the Vine,
page 22

Sailboat **from** *Children's Wallhanging*, **page 26**

Kite from *Children's Wallhanging,* **page 26**

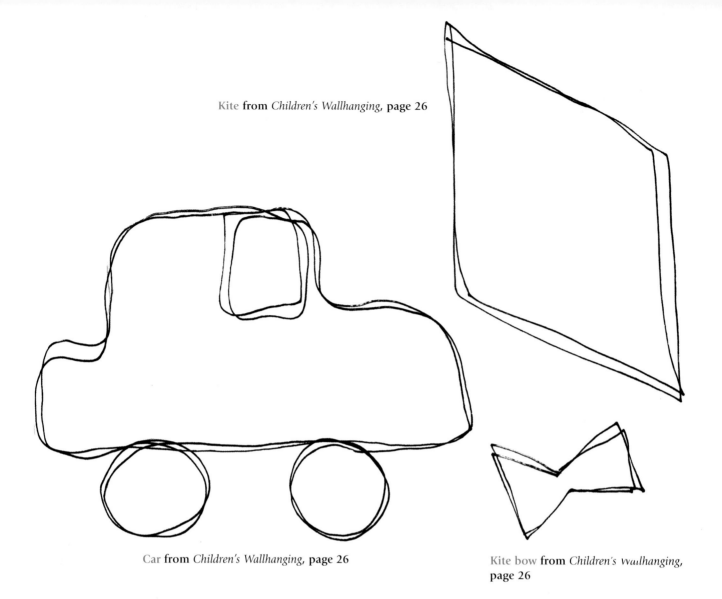

Car from *Children's Wallhanging,* **page 26**

Kite bow from *Children's Wallhanging,* **page 26**

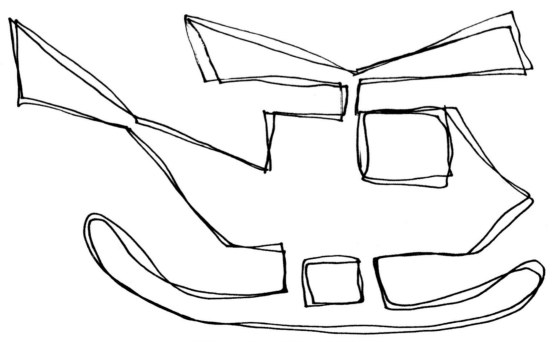

Helicopter from *Children's Wallhanging,* **page 26**

Bear from *Children's Wallhanging,*
page 26

Boy from *Children's
Wallhanging,* page 26

Girl from *Children's Wallhanging,* page 26

Holly and berries **from**
Christmas Table Runner **and**
Christmas Placemat, **page 32**

Presents **from** *Christmas Table Runner*, **page 32**

Presents **from** *Christmas Table Runner*, **page 32**

Presents **from** *Christmas Table Runner*, **page 32**

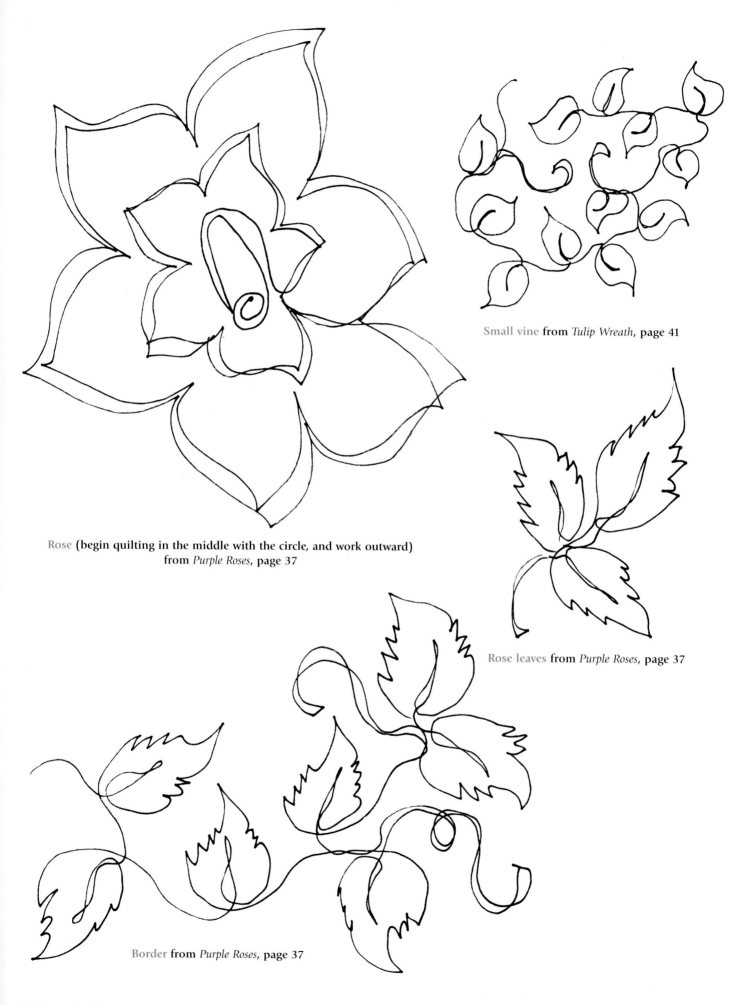

Small vine **from** *Tulip Wreath*, **page 41**

Rose **(begin quilting in the middle with the circle, and work outward)**
from *Purple Roses*, **page 37**

Rose leaves **from** *Purple Roses*, **page 37**

Border **from** *Purple Roses*, **page 37**

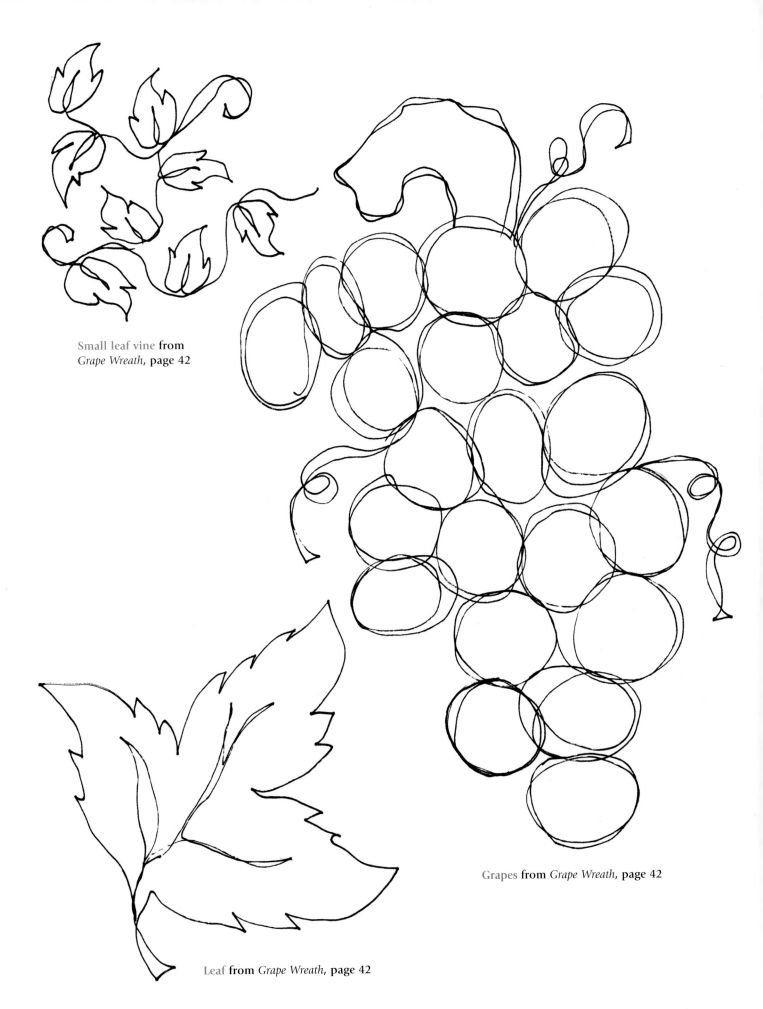

Small leaf vine from
Grape Wreath, **page 42**

Grapes from *Grape Wreath*, **page 42**

Leaf from *Grape Wreath*, **page 42**

Feathered wreath **from** *Striply Speaking,* **page 39**

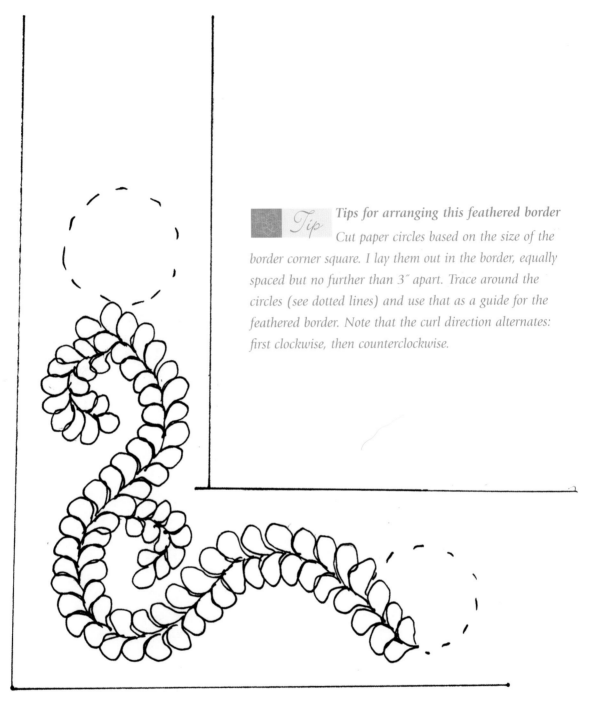

Tips for arranging this feathered border
Cut paper circles based on the size of the border corner square. I lay them out in the border, equally spaced but no further than 3″ apart. Trace around the circles (see dotted lines) and use that as a guide for the feathered border. Note that the curl direction alternates: first clockwise, then counterclockwise.

Feathered border **from** *Striply Speaking,* **page 39**

Flowers and leaves **from** *President's Quilt #1,* **page 38**

Poinsettia and holly leaves **from** *Happy Holidays*, **page 40**

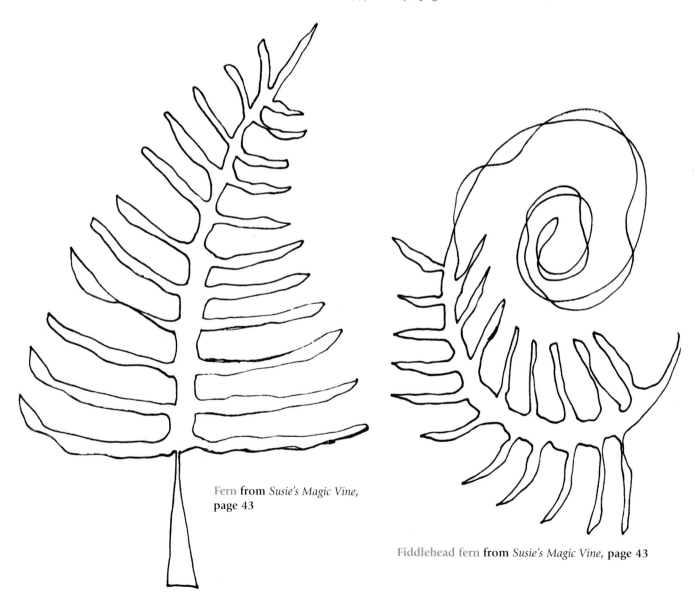

HAPPY HOLIDAYS

Letters **from** *Happy Holidays,* **page 40**

Fern **from** *Susie's Magic Vine,*
page 43

Fiddlehead fern **from** *Susie's Magic Vine,* **page 43**

About the Author

Kathy Sandbach lives in the Pacific Northwest, where the sound of the ocean can be heard, the view of a small lake out the back windows is heaven, and the cool weather is perfect! She has taught machine quilting since 1986. This is her third book. The mother of two grown children, Kathy enjoys spending time with them and lecturing, teaching, and traveling. Visit her website at www.machinequiltlady.com.

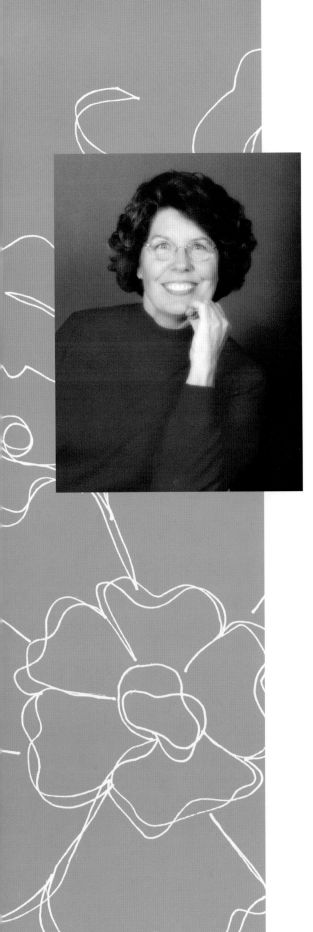

Resources

Forget-Me-Knot
640 2nd Street SE (Highway 101)
Bandon, OR
(800) 347-9021
michelle@forget-me-knots.net

Quilt Gripper Gloves
(303) 838-5122
toni_fitzwater@msn.com

Susie Robbins
Susie's Magic Vine pattern
NelsonSueRob@comcast.net

That Thread Shop
P.O. Box 325
Lemont, IL
(708) 301-3172
www.thatthreadshop.com

Threads That Bind
120 Central Avenue
Coos Bay, OR
(541) 267-0749
threads@harborside.com

Index

Subject Index

Quilting Designs Index

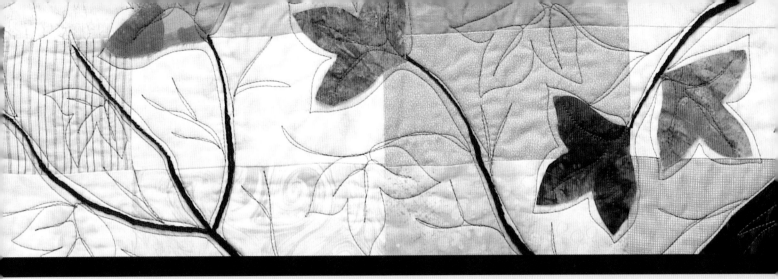

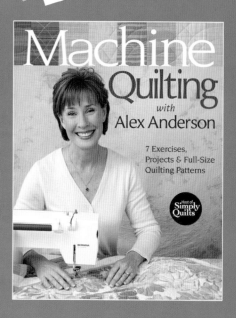
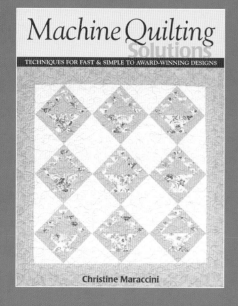
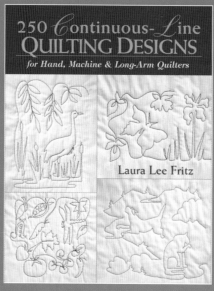

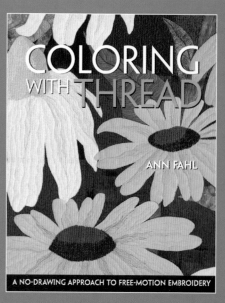